Dark Reality

Understanding And Guarding Against The True Nature Of People, Their Self Serving Intentions, And Their Hidden Agendas

By Virginia Smith

I0423316

Copyright 2016 by Virginia Smith

Published by Make Profits Easy LLC

Profitsdaily123@aol.com

facebook.com/MakeProfitsEasy

Table of Contents

INTRODUCTION: THE DARK REALITY AROUND US

The other day I was Face Timing with a friend I hadn't talked to in a long time. We talked for a while about various mutual friends, life, and the latest season of America's Got Talent. Then I asked her where she was working these days, and she started telling me about this pyramid scheme job she had started last winter.

Before I quite realized what was happening, she was asking me if her job sounded like something I wanted to do or if her products sounded like something I wanted to invest in. Suddenly, I felt lied to, like this friend only decided to renew her acquaintance with me in order to sell me something.

The bait and switch left me feeling cheated.

Not too long ago, I was talking with some friends who were discussing the merits of Facebook and other social media sites.

"I think it's crazy awesome that they don't make us pay to sign up for an account," my friend Anna said.

The others murmured their agreement and went on to talk about the value of having a live stream of their high school classmates' wedding photos at their fingertips.

Then my cynical friend, Zelda, piped up and said, "If you aren't paying for the product, then *you* are the product."

Her words took a moment to sink in. Everyone grew quiet.

"How do you figure?" Ben, the most calculating of my friends said.

"Advertisers are the ones paying to post their banners all over the social media sites. Everything we've ever googled is used to determine which ads we see. The social media sites aren't giving us a service; they are selling us to advertising companies who want to get us to buy things from them. It works, too. All of you have bought something that you saw in an ad on Facebook."

Anna and Ben fell silent, studying Zelda dubiously. Zelda didn't flinch or fidget. She never did. She gazed from one face to the next, until her eyes rested on mine.

"There's always a hidden agenda," Zelda said. "That's the dark reality."

Back in college, I met a very charming man in my intro to philosophy class. The first day of class was the morning after I broke up with my boyfriend of three years. I walked into class two minutes late with splotchy skin and puffy eyes.

After class, Charlie sidled up to me and asked me what was wrong. He complimented me effusively and bought me lunch at a little hipster coffee shop down the street from my apartment. We were instant friends.

My naïve college self couldn't fathom why any guy would ever take advantage of me, so the thought never crossed my mind, even weeks later when he started making hints about wanting to sleep together.

I kept laughing off his comments, at first believing that he was joking, but gradually the lighthearted sexual innuendos turned into biting little comments like, "If you're looking for a way to repay me for all of the lunches I've paid for and tears I've mopped up for you..."

I started to feel guilty for laughing him off and saying no. After all, he had put up with a lot of tears and paid for a lot of lunches. Besides, he always made me feel so good with his little compliments about how pretty I was and how good I was at dancing. I did think he was attractive, and he seemed like he was really into me. What harm could it do?

Eventually, I gave in.

He was a terrible lover, only going so far as to satisfy himself with very little thought for how he was making me feel and whether I was able to finish. The first time I slept with him, the event lasted for about seven minutes in total, and then he was zipping up his jeans and dashing out of my apartment.

The relationship went on for several months. He'd call me late at night and invite himself over to my place, and I always let him in. He was still charming, but instead of listening, he started shushing me and moving in for kisses and gropes instead.

One night I pointed out to him that we never talked about anything anymore.

He only grinned at me and said, "You and I are beyond words, don't you think?"

I wasn't stupid. I had an inkling that the reason we never talked anymore was because I was no longer his friend but the call girl for when he needed to get laid. My friends at the time even told me as much. Still, he was very charming, and was flattered that someone as hot and sought after as he was would come to me for his late night needs.

The wakeup call came when I was out dancing one Saturday night with my girlfriends and I saw him there at the club with another girl.

Anna said, "Is that Charlie?" Her voice dripped with disgust.

I was so embarrassed. And angry. I walked up to him and pulled his arm until he faced me.

He grinned. "Hey," he said, winking at me. "What's up?" He put an arm around the girl next to him. "Have you met my girlfriend, Daphne?"

"Girlfriend?" I said. "I didn't know you had a girlfriend. If I had known that, I wouldn't have..." I let my words trail off. He had already turned away from me.

Daphne looked from me to him and then turned a cold shoulder on me.

Later that week, Charlie called me to ask if he could come over.

"Did you break up with your girlfriend?" I asked.

"No, but it's all good. She can't keep up with all of my needs anyway," he said. "Besides, it never mattered to you before."

Rather than argue with him, I hung up and called Zelda, my dark-hearted friend whose cynicism was only outdone by her loyalty.

"I knew he was an ass," she said. She then called around to all of our friends until she found Daphne's number, and she texted her every bad thing she could think of about Daphne's good for nothing skanky boyfriend, Charlie.

This book about these stories and many more. People are complicated, selfish creatures, and while a few people in your life might genuinely have your best interests in mind and heart, most of the world couldn't care less about you.

Everyone has hidden agendas. Everyone is selfish. No matter where you are or what you do, there's always someone ready to take advantage of your generosity, kind nature, or vulnerabilities.

This book is a wakeup call. It is also a tool to help you understand the ins and outs of intentions and hidden agendas and to give you some pointers that will help you guard against them.

There's an old African proverb that says, "Beware of a naked man who offers you a shirt." Consider this book to be the metaphorical shirt delivered safely into your hands.

CHAPTER ONE: ON HUMAN NATURE, SELF LOVE, AND OTHER MOTIVATIONS

My mother was diagnosed with breast cancer the summer after I graduated from college. Since my older sister had a job and a husband and kids, and my brother was away in Africa on a mission's trip, I was the logical choice to move back in with my parents and make sure they were taken care of. After all, I hadn't been able to secure a job yet, and I had all kinds of free time while I applied for jobs and went to one job interview after another.

As my mother went to chemotherapy and radiation, lost her hair, and eventually had to get a mastectomy, I watched my father's health deteriorate as well. He stopped exercising and going out with his buddies after work. Every second of his free time was spent either with my mother or worrying about her.

I told him I was there to help him care for her so that he could have a break, and he kept telling me, "I vowed to take care of her in sickness and in health. *Sickness*. This is sickness."

Nothing I said seemed to make a difference. I saw him growing old before my eyes. And I saw, too, that my mother's worry also grew. She didn't worry about herself. "I know I'm going to get through this," she said, "but I'm not sure your father will. I don't know how to help him."

On a cool fall evening, some of my parents' friends came over for dinner. One of the friends took my father aside after the meal. I didn't mean to eavesdrop, but I was caught with my foot an inch above the squeaky stair, and I sensed that this might be the conversation I'd tried for four months to have with my father, and I didn't want to disrupt it. I held my breath and stilled my leg in midair.

"Edward, I know you love your wife, and you would do anything to help her get better," the friend said.

My father murmured his agreement.

"You need to start taking care of yourself. That's what she needs from you right now."

My father let out a string of protests, but something in the friend's expression must have stopped him.

"You're on the verge of making yourself sick, and it's stressing Justine out and keeping her from focusing on her own recovery."

"I'm so worried about her," my father said.

A moment of silence passed, during which I wished I could see what was happening. Then, "Your daughter moved back in to help out so that you could still have time to take care of yourself. Don't make her put her life on hold even longer by making yourself sick."

Another long silence followed. My lungs ached from the breath I was holding. I slowly let it out, struggling to keep it from leaving me in a giant loud gust.

"Let's go jogging tomorrow morning like we used to. We can go early and be back in time for you to see to Justine before you go to work."

My father agreed.

In order to survive as a species, our minds are wired for a certain level of self-love that ensures that we follow the promptings of our physiology—we eat when we're hungry, we sleep when we're tired, and we eliminate waste when our large intestines and bladders are full. When we fail to do these basic things, we eventually render ourselves useless both to ourselves and to those around us.

The story about my father sounds like the sweet story of a happily married couple, but it's also a look at the dark side of what can happen when a person forgets to demonstrate a basic level of self-love.

Sometimes we hear the word self-love and immediately assume that having self-love makes us selfish. An overinflated sense of self-worth can certainly become selfish, but self-love, in its essence, is about caring for ourselves to such a level that we are in a position to extend care to others. To stop caring for yourself is to, however inadvertently, stop caring for others.

A step beyond physiological needs, we also groom ourselves to make ourselves attractive to others and participate in communities in order to make money, be productive, and win affection and adulation from our peers and authority figures. In moderation, these are natural, healthy things for us to desire and pursue. Without these things, we lose interest in the world and turn into our own worst enemies.

Self-love motivates us to take care of ourselves, and lack of it allows us to let others take advantage of us, but there are many other motivations that drive the way people think, speak, and behave.

Different Kinds of Motives

People always want something, and what they do is a direct result of that want. A want creates some kind of motive that propels a person to act. The following are possible motives that people have that can foster the dark reality around us. Keep in mind as you read that the motives themselves aren't necessarily dark, but, blanketed by harmful intentions, they can be lethal.

Power

A small town's plastics factory provides jobs for 75 percent of the town's citizens. The owner of the factory decides to run for city council, so that he can have a bigger say in how the town is run and more power over the individual lives of the townspeople.

In order to win the election, he informs the townspeople that if they don't vote for him, half of their jobs at the factory will have to be sent overseas, because the other candidates who are running against him are against big businesses and will vote to tax the factory so hard that there will be no other option.

Will the other candidates running for city council actually vote against the best interests of 75 percent of the town's people if they are elected? Probably not, but the factory owner has used his already powerful position in the town as leverage to create a scenario in which people either vote for him or risk losing their jobs. It's a nasty power move motivated by a desire for greater power.

The factory owner in this scenario is motivated to run for the city council by his desire for increased power. There are many people who are motivated by power; some power-hungry dictators come to mind, as do abusive family members who find pleasure in exerting control over the people in their lives they are closest to. Power can motivate on a large scale or a small scale.

Achievement

I used to have a friend, we'll call him Fred, who was so focused on achieving his goal of being the youngest and brightest person to ever be internationally recognized for his stellar work in the field of theoretical physics that he would go to any lengths to reach his dream. Fred didn't care about anything as much as he cared about his goals. His quest for the Nobel Prize became his idol, and everything else was subservient to that goal.

He didn't go home for his grandfather's funeral. He didn't return phones calls. He didn't do favors for friends. He didn't think about anyone's needs but his own. He ate when he was hungry and never offered to grab anything for anyone else while he got his own food. He constantly talked about the latest breakthrough he was being recognized for. He didn't have time to listen to anything not relevant to his own achievement trajectory.

One night, during winter break, my junky car broke down on the side of the road. Zelda and I were on our way back from the Laundromat in what had suddenly turned into an ice storm. I had exhausted my knowledge of cars as soon as I managed to open the hood of my car. It was below freezing cold, and, like broke college students, neither of us had money to pay for a tow truck. Fred was the only friend we knew who was still in town during the long break, so we called him for help.

"He's not going to answer," Zelda said.

I was more optimistic. "He has to see that I'm calling eventually. No one who's okay calls and leaves twelve voicemails and sixteen texts. He'll call back."

But he didn't.

Instead, we called the only number we could think of: 9-1-1.

I later asked Fred why he didn't respond to my messages.

"Theoretical physics doesn't solve itself," he said.

We were no longer friends after that.

Security

Security has become something of a developed world craze. I can think of several friends off the top of my head who base most of their life decisions on what they think will bring them the greatest amount of safety and security in life, whether that's physically, financially, or relationally. They will take a corporate job they loathe, befriend people they dislike, and wear a helmet whenever they leave the house if it means that they can gain and maintain security in their lives.

These are not the people you call when you need an investor for your startup or a complete overhaul of your company's business plan. These are the people who will play it safe regardless of the people who stand to gain something by making a change that could alter the status quo.

Social Affiliation

My friend Anna moved out to Los Angeles after college to become an actress, but more than becoming an actress, she wanted to meet famous actors and actresses. Like most struggling actors, she got a job as a waitress in the fanciest restaurant that would hire her. She was constantly sending off postcards detailing the famous people she had seen or met at her job.

It was pretty neat to hear about her experiences, but that didn't make it any less annoying when she skipped another friend's wedding in order to hang out with some random actor acquaintance she'd met at the club who had promised to take a look at her head shots.

People who are motivated by social affiliation tend to seek out experiences that allow them to hobnob with the elite and ingratiate themselves with those of high status.

Status or Prestige

While some people are motivated by knowing and being known by the elite, others are motivated by becoming the elite. These people might place a lot of value on being able to dress the part; owning the right gadgets, jewelry, and vehicles; and living in the best homes.

For a couple of years in middle school I went to a fancy boarding school in England on a need-based scholarship. The school was great, but the kids who went there thrived on flaunting their parents' fortunes with the latest purses and hats and the best cell phones, and the signed advanced reader copies of books that wouldn't come out for six more months.

The worst insult I could give to these kids was my total ignorance of all of the emblems of status that they touted, and they hated me for my blank stares and utter lack of education when it came to understanding the difference between the rich kids and the filthy rich kids.

Curiosity

My friend Zelda has an insatiable curiosity that sometimes borders on the sick and manipulative. She'll argue a point with a very defensive person just to see how long it takes him to get angry with her and lose his cool. She'll stare at a stranger on the train to see how long it takes her to comment. She'll play devil's advocate just to figure out how much someone has thought through their brilliant new strategy.

One time, back when we had just become roommates, Zelda hid all of my shoes in her bedroom for the pleasure of watching me wander around the apartment in total confusion and to see how long it would take me to either ask her or check her bedroom. She even timed me with a stopwatch.

Her curiosity wasn't always harmless. I'd have to take off my shoes to count the number of times she started an argument between dating and married couples just to see how they handled conflict with each other. A couple of them actually broke up.

"Don't you feel bad?" I asked her.

"No. If a little disagreement was all it took to break them up, then there was far more trouble in their relationship than I could have possibly been the cause of."

I'm sure there are some possible motives that I've missed, but these give you an overview of the some of the more likely culprits. Keep in mind that while people act based on what motivates them, they aren't always motivated by one primary thing. Many people carry around a mix of motives that fluctuates based on the situation. A person who is motivated by social affiliation with wealthy socialites might become intrigued with emblems of status, and their primary motivation can shift.

Likewise, one might be motivated both by power and curiosity, an exceptionally manipulative, scary combination. This might be a powerful dictator whose morbid curiosity drives him to treat people and their lives like toys to be messed with just to see what will happen.

While I've spun these motivations in a dark light, they aren't in and of themselves dark and destructive. After all, you can let your motives dictate your actions, or you can note your motivations and then choose your actions. We all have that choice.

There's a saying that goes, "Who you are in secret is who you really are." But who is to say what your innermost self consists of? Who you are in public is how others perceive you, and often that's far more important when it comes to participating in a social world. That's what the next chapter is about.

CHAPTER TWO: THE EDGE OF INFERENCE AND INTENTION

A few years ago I worked for a Fortune 500 company, which will remain unnamed, and the whole time I was there I had the distinct impression that my boss hated me from the first time she laid eyes on me. I came in for my training on day one, and introduced myself to her full of excitement and gratitude about the new adventure I was embarking on.

My boss gave me the up-down and said, "I wasn't the one who hired you, so don't thank me."

Her tone was carefully neutral, and I sat down at the conference table feeling confused. I mentally reviewed the interaction for anything in my own demeanor that might have offended her. I checked my teeth discreetly in my compact mirror. I made sure my clothing was covering me properly. Everything seemed to be in place.

Perhaps I had imagined my impression of her disgust.

I worked hard to learn the job quickly and perform it better and faster than anyone else on my floor, and still the boss didn't seem to like me. She'd ask for volunteers to work on extra projects, and though I'd offer, she would ignore me and volunteer someone who wasn't interested.

"Why doesn't she like you?" my coworkers asked on multiple occasions like this.

I had no idea.

Finally, after another rude brush-off by the boss, I approached her and asked to speak with her privately. I asked her if she found something about my work to be unsatisfactory or if I had offended her in any way.

She smiled at me indulgently and told me I was being ridiculous. She turned her attention to her computer and ignored me until I eventually let myself out of her office.

"It's because you're a woman of color," one of my coworkers said one day.

"That doesn't make any sense. So is she," I said.

"That's why she doesn't like you. She worked hard to get where she is, and she doesn't want someone just like her to come in and replace her," he said. "I'm not taking her side; I'm just explaining."

I watched her closely over the next few weeks and silently tested the theory. I noticed that she gave more opportunities to men and white women than she did to the few other women of color in the office. I asked these women if they were noticing the same things I was. They also admitted that they never felt like she liked them, though they didn't know why.

"Sometimes people just don't like you, you know?" one coworker said. "You can't win them all."

I pointed out the thing that we had in common—our skin color. No sooner were the words out of my mouth, that I heard my name barked from twelve feet away. It was the boss.

I followed her back to her office, this time filled with dread. I'd finally given her something to dislike me for. I should have kept my mouth shut.

She wrote me up for making discriminatory comments in the workplace. Over the next couple of weeks, she pled her case to her superiors, and then they called me in to speak my piece. I told them my version of the story, but whatever version she had said to them had already persuaded them to fire me. I packed my desk up and was out of there before lunch, while she smirked at me from across the floor.

Defining Perception and Inference

Perception is the ability to see, hear, taste, touch, smell, and understand our reality. It is how we form our intuition and lend it credibility.

Inference is a conclusion that we draw based on evidence and reasoning. Our perceptions directly influence our inferences.

Our ability to perceive and then infer is one of our greatest assets as humans. When we see fire, we infer that it's hot, and that we shouldn't touch it. When we see someone do one thing and hear them say the opposite, we infer that they are hypocrites and we can't trust them. When someone ignores us or passes us over for a promotion, we infer that they don't like us.

Inference is an educated guess based on evidence that we have collected through our intuition and senses. I inferred that my boss didn't like me based on the way she treated me and then confirmed this by noting the insulting way in which she had gotten me fired.

An inference isn't always correct, however, because human perception is prone to error. Because people are so different from each other and carry their own likes, dislikes, and prejudices, there's often a vast difference between perception and intention. Just because you perceive something doesn't mean that it's reality at its truest.

For example, just because you think someone hates you doesn't mean that they actually hate you. This sounds like a "duh" statement, but hear me out. In my case, I was right, but it might have been a different story if I had showed up to my first day of work assuming that my boss would hate me because I'm part Mexican and part Native American. Arriving with a chip on my shoulder might have created a self-fulfilling prophecy, or, at the very least, it might have colored my perception of my boss's reactions and intentions towards me. I might have taken her passing me over for one extra assignment as reinforcement of my preconceived notions. I might have assumed that she didn't smile at me in the halls in passing because she disliked me instead of assuming that she didn't smile because she was busy or because I didn't smile first.

We infer a lot about a person based on their words, behaviors, and demeanors. Sometimes we hit the nail on the head; sometimes we pound our own thumbs. At the end of the day, all we have is our best guess and our logical reasoning skills.

Often our inferences are projections of our own feelings. One time I was in the grocery store browsing the peanut butter aisle when a cart smashed into the backs of my heels. I turned and saw an elderly woman grimacing. "Watch where you're going," I said, glaring back at her. I continued down the aisle and then heard a jar crash on the floor. I turned in time to see the woman slumping over her cart and crumpling to the ground. The cart skidded forward, slowing her fall.

That was when I realized that what I had perceived to be a spiteful, elderly woman in a hurry was actually a sick woman having a serious health crisis. I ran to the woman to keep her from falling into the broken glass and then called 9-1-1 in a guilty panic.

On the other hand, we might perceive a person to be good and honorable when they are merely making pains to look that way in order to get something from us.

A sales associate as a car dealership might become super chummy with you in order to sell you a brand new vehicle for more than your stated budget. He might ingratiate himself into your life by asking you questions about your preferences, family, and needs. He might share some of his own personal experiences in order to build an illusion of friendship.

When he has you laughing and chatting with him like you're old buddies, he shows you the vehicle he wants you to buy, explaining how it meets your stated needs. He might even be apologetic about the fact that it's above your budget and then justify the purchase by saying that, after all, it's something you only buy once every ten years or so, and it's important that all of your family's needs are met.

Before you know it, you are happily signing a lease on a vehicle you can't quite afford and driving off the lot with a lemon that breaks down a week later.

The Novel

You've probably read books that flip back and forth between multiple perspectives before. The characters essentially take turns sharing their own perspectives with the reader, giving us a well-rounded view of how the situation actually is. Life is kind of like that. We are all players in a narrative that keeps on going.

It's a bit of a false dichotomy to say that there are two sides to a story. In fact, there are as many sides to a story are there are people in the story. Even identical twins living identical lives can perceive an event in a different way.

For example, you might feel that you're being selfish for taking some time alone for yourself over the weekend to recharge instead of going to your sister's Pampered Chef party, and she might make you feel like the worst, most unsupportive sibling for missing it. However, you know your needs better than she does. Perhaps it is selfish of her to expect you to give up the only evening you have off from work and childrearing every week to go to a party designed to pressure you into buying things.

An argument could be made either way. It is entirely a matter of perception and the manner in which the story is spun.

The differences in perception aren't always blatant and opposite. Often they are subtle. You and I might be caught in the midst of an armed robbery while we're at the bank and both think it's terrible, but we might not be able to agree on whether or not it's ridiculous how long it's taking to be rescued or the level of fierceness of the armed robbers. I might perceive the robbers to be like nervous kids brandishing dangerous weapons; you might perceive them as ferocious men with calculating gazes under their masks.

Past experiences, social class, age, ethnicity, and any number of other factors feed into our perspectives and perceptions of the world around us, and that's important to keep in mind whenever you are analyzing a situation or a person.

CHAPTER THREE: THE MANY SHADES OF SELFISHNESS

Beyond the necessity of self-love, people are capable of a wide range of selfishness that varies in degree and magnitude. Most of us have experienced several, or even all, of these at some point in our lives. Think back to the last time you made a selfish decision or acted in a selfish manner. I promise you've done it before. It's the human inclination.

However, it is important to distinguish between a person who acts selfishly sometimes and a selfish person. While most of us act in a selfish manner from time to time, not all of us base every decision be make out of pure selfishness. There are people whose go-to decision is the selfish one. The latter is what this chapter is about.

Types of Selfishness

The Shotgun

The Shotgun is the girl who always calls dibs on the best thing and goes out of her way to beat you to it, whether it's the front passenger shotgun seat, the biggest chicken wing in the takeout container, or the grandest office in the building. She is the queen of dibs.

Geoffrey grew up as the oldest in a very competitive family. He called dibs and won most of the time by nature of being the oldest, fastest, and strongest of his siblings. Whenever a sibling beat him to the most sought after seat in the car or the biggest piece of cake, he pouted and couldn't understand why his parents allowed such an injustice to take place.

As an adult, Geoffrey hasn't changed much. He feels entitled to have what he asks for. It honestly doesn't occur to him that others might want or deserve something more than he does. He believes that wanting something is a good enough reason for him to get it.

The Hoarder

The Hoarder takes the last piece of cake just to have it, even if he will only eat half of it. He takes the sack of free clothes that you've put in your donation pile even if they aren't in his size and he will never wear them. He's not the person who asks if anyone wants the leftover cupcakes before taking them, or if he does, he'll do so only after he's already claimed them so that it would be in bad taste for anyone to object.

I met a guy once whose house was filled to the brim with clothes he never wore. He was a work acquaintance who was supposed to host a work party for some foreign guests, and he'd asked for some assistance with tidying his house before the big night. I volunteered to help.

When I arrived, I noted that there wasn't a single surface inside the place that wasn't covered in stacks of clothing. I asked why he kept so many clothes.

"It's wasteful to just throw them out," he said, like this should have been obvious to me.

"You could donate them," I said.

"They're mine. Why would I do that?" he asked, like this, too, should have been obvious to me.

"Do you wear them all?" I asked.

"You're kidding me, right?" he said. He provided no further explanation.

I helped him move the clothing to other rooms of the house to free up the dining room, but after a few hours, it became apparent that the rooms needed more work than a little bit of rearranging and tidying. I instead let everyone know that I could host the dinner at my house. My house was smaller, but at least I hadn't filled my dining room with enough clothes to clothe half of a third world nation.

If this example seems ridiculous, it's because this brand of selfishness is equally ridiculous. It's like the woman who decides to date a guy she doesn't really like because she knows that if she doesn't, he will find someone else, and she can't stand that idea.

The Leech

The Leech is the soul-sucking fiend who will take everything you give her and more and have no clue how much havoc she is reeking in your life. She takes everything you've got and still demands more with no regard for how her needs are cutting into yours and keeping you from being able to function in a normal, healthy manner.

My friend Helen had just been dumped by her cheating, no-good boyfriend, and a bunch of us had gone over to her house to give her moral support while she kicked him out and then to throw her a Freedom Party, as was our tradition whenever a friend had a very bad breakup.

Midway through the party, our leeching friend, Izzy, showed up, bemoaning the fact that she had just dumped the guy she was seeing too, and she understood better than anyone what Helen was going through. Unsure if Izzy was seriously comparing her voluntary two-weekend fling with Helen's four-year emotionally abusive relationship, we watched her in horror as she continued to talk. Before we realized what was happening, Izzy had broken down in uncontrollable sobs, and Helen was doing her best to comfort her.

Zelda was the first to spring to action. Sneering, she said, "Izzy, this party isn't about you. If you can't handle that, then you should leave."

Izzy blinked, looked around at all of us, and said, "You don't understand real suffering. I've been through so much. I can't help it if that makes me a complicated person to know."

Zelda snorted.

Izzy heaved a dramatic sigh, made a show of sucking down a huge sob, and left the party. If we weren't going to let her leech away at Helen, then she wasn't interested.

The Inconsiderate

The Inconsiderate makes everything all about him. Your mother may have just died, but he's asking you why you didn't return his call and demanding to know how you thought that made *him* feel. The mark of the Inconsiderate is him complete and utter lack of empathy. He feels only his own pain and joy and has no ability or inclination to vex himself over yours.

During Helen's Freedom Party, Helen's ex-boyfriend came back claiming to have left something in the medicine cabinet. He stormed into the kitchen, and a couple of the guys placed themselves between him and Helen.

Then he starting ranting about how unfair all of this was. "You have no idea what you're doing to me," he yelled at Helen. "I have to move back in with my parents. Do you know how hard it is for a guy to get laid when he lives with his parents? Plus, some of my friends are blaming me for this. You know it's more your fault than mine. If you hadn't gotten that work promotion and started being too tired for sex, then I never would have looked elsewhere for it. You are selfish. You've never thought about my needs and how I was affected by your selfish choices. You've always put your career ahead of me, and I deserve better than that."

Coming from a guy who belittled every decision she ever made, tried to isolate her from her friends even though he himself went out every night, and flew into selfish jealous rages whenever she mentioned a male friend's name, this was highly inconsiderate. If we hadn't already hated the guy, we were more than ready to do so at that moment, seeing up close and personal the extent to which he never thought about anyone but himself.

When he left, Helen broke down in sobs. "He's right. I'm selfish, and I took that promotion without asking him if it was okay."

"No," I said. "If he loved you, he would have been happy for you. If loyalty and faithfulness had mattered to him, he would have started helping you out with more things around the house so that you had time for him. This is not on you."

And it wasn't, because there's only so much you can do for an Inconsiderate before they transform into a Leech.

The Self-Deprecator

Like the Inconsiderate, the Self-Deprecator makes everything about himself. Unlike the Inconsiderate, he is overly engrossed in his own flaws and problems, however miniscule they may be. No matter what you say, he has something worse to top that. You're having a bad hair day? He has a zit the size of Texas on his nose. You failed a calculus exam? He failed the class. You got fired? He got fired once, and it was way worse.

With the Self-Deprecator, it's always like a sick sort of competition to be around him.

Sometimes the Self-Deprecator can appear to be an extraordinarily humble person at first glance. I had a friend in high school who was constantly beating herself up over the tiniest detail, and she couldn't take a compliment to save her soul. At first it was endearing, like all of those "she don't know she's beautiful" songs that are so popular these days.

But the more time I spent around her, the more I realized that her humility was false. She berated herself because it got her attention. If she said she was fat, four other people were usually around to tell her that she was skinny and beautiful. If she said she was stupid, there was always someone there who knew that she was in the top ten percent of the class.

All of the insults and derogatory comments she heaped on herself when she was with others were actually thinly veiled attempts at winning affirmation and attention. Around the time I stopped giving her the answers she was fishing for, she stopped hanging out with me, which I don't think was a coincidence.

The Narcissist

The narcissist is one of the worst types of selfish people. Her only genuine interest lies in herself, talking about herself, and hearing others talk about her. She gets bored when other people talk about themselves or other subjects that interest them and often knows innumerable ways to bring the conversation back to her. She strives to always be the center of attention, and if one audience won't let her take center stage, she'll find a new audience.

For a brief time, I knew someone who worked in show business. I wouldn't say we were friends, because while I knew far more than I wanted to about him, he knew nothing about me. I was just that familiar head he talked at, but for some reason he really liked me and went out of his way to see me. This confused me greatly, since I knew that he must know a lot of people in his profession.

Then I met some of his colleagues, and I instantly understood why he didn't like them. They were just like he was—vain, self-absorbed, ignorant, and completely uninterested in anyone but themselves. I could be having the worst day in the world with mascara running everywhere, and he would talk on about himself without even noticing that I was in distress. The day I got fired from the Fortune 500 company, he showed up at my house and passed half an hour in blissful ignorance before I finally got sick of him and asked him to leave.

"I'm going through something, right now, and you haven't even noticed," I said.

He looked completely baffled. "I'm telling you about my new costume and I feel like you don't even care," he said in response.

"You know what," I said, "today I don't care. I just got fired from my job, and I need someone to listen to me. I don't want to hear any more about your costume or why you think the sleeves should be longer, and if I hear one more word out of your mouth about it, I'm going to scream."

"Didn't you listen to me at all? I'm not talking about the sleeves; I'm talking about the belt loops."

I screamed. And I continued screaming until he had gotten up and let himself out the front door.

The Devil

The Devil steals your lover without apology. She spends your paycheck without asking and has no thought for your carefully planned budget designed to help you save for a down payment on a functional car next fall. She doesn't care about the difference between her wants and your needs. She will do whatever it takes to get her way, and she will fight you tooth and nail until you back down or let her destroy you.

Many selfish people act selfishly out of ignorance; the Devil is not one of those selfish people. Often, she knows what she's doing. She has the cognitive complexity to see that what she's doing causes damage to those around her. She has the means to stop herself from doing what she's doing and the intelligence to know that her actions and words are morally reprehensible.

She doesn't care.

I haven't met many Devils in my lifetime, and only one I would consider to be a true Devil.

His reputation was so bad it curdled my blood just hearing about the things he'd done. He'd raped naïve college girls, swindled elderly people out of hundreds of thousands of dollars, and bombed an elementary school just to see his name on the news.

I met him a couple of short weeks before the school bombing got him locked away when I was browsing the staple guns at the hardware store. He wasn't handsome, per se, but he had a charisma that I found to be initially intriguing. I introduced myself to him on a whim, and the way he smiled made my insides shudder. I later learned that that feeling had been dread, but at the time, I had mistaken it for excitement and agreed to meet him for dinner that evening.

Unlike a lot of the men I'd gone out with to that point, he asked the questions and listened to my answers. Whenever I turned the spotlight on him, he gave a quick answer and flipped it back on me. I thought he was being gentlemanly. It didn't occur to me that he was pumping me for information. Since I had walked to the restaurant, I let him drive me home after our date.

When we got to my house, he asked if he could come in for a nightcap. Still blissfully ignorant of anything amiss, I graciously invited him in and got down the glasses. No sooner had I turned my back on him, than he was behind me, pressing a warm, hard object into the small of my back. I'm humiliated to remember that I laughed at first, thinking that he was simply turned on and playing with me.

Then I heard a click, and the hard object pressed hard enough into my back that I felt the round barrel of the gun. Adrenaline flashed through me and zipped along my spine. "What are you doing?" I asked.

"Don't move, or I will shoot you," he said. He attached my wrists with zip ties to the slats of the cupboards above my head where my hand still lingered holding the two wine glasses in midair. "Drop the glasses."

I hesitated. They had been a present from my grandmother, and I knew they had not been cheap.

"Drop them." He raised the gun to my temple.

I let them drop to the floor, wincing at the shatter that followed.

He tied a rag across my mouth and then my eyes, pulling the knots tight so that my chapped lips cracked painfully at how widely they were stretched.

Everything happened so quickly and unexpectedly that I didn't have time to scream or to struggle.

I heard him rummaging somewhere in the living room. I heard him toying with the safe I kept there. A few minutes later, after what had felt like hours, all was silent. I tried to struggle against the zip ties, but they cut into my wrists instead of coming lose or breaking. Zelda came home a couple of hours later and undid me. We called 9-1-1 and searched the house for everything he'd taken, finding that he'd made off with all of the jewelry and cash in my safe and swiped the antique sewing machine that my grandmother had given me for my fourteenth birthday.

Zelda searched him online and found that I was one of his lucky victims. "He once killed a taxi driver who tried to make him pay for his ride," she said.

CHAPTER FOUR: GUARDING AGAINST SELFISH PEOPLE

The last chapter was chalk full of stories about selfishness, and this chapter is the antidote. In it, you will find practical techniques for shutting down selfish people and their behavior and, when all else fails, shutting them out of your life completely.

Obviously you won't be able to cut every selfish person out of your life. That would be hugely impractical and not entirely necessary or healthy, especially given that everyone is selfish from time to time, including you.

That being said, this chapter will provide you with some useful ideas for protecting yourself from rampant selfishness and shutting down those who would selfishly take advantage of you. This chapter also provides techniques for dealing with selfish behavior in the event that there's no real solution for it.

Evaluate

Honestly evaluate the situation. Are they being selfish? Are you the one being selfish? How much of your perception is projection and how much is inference based in subjective evidence rather than objective evidence? Is there any reason why you might perceive them to be more or less selfish than they are actually being?

Sometimes it's easy to let your own emotions cloud a situation. When I'm angry with my brother, I always perceive his actions to be a lot more selfish than they actually are. When we were kids, I would assume he was being selfish for not giving me a ride to school in the morning and making me take the bus, when the reality was that he planned to be at school an hour early for math help, and he knew I wouldn't want to get up in time to go with him. He didn't always explain this to me, and I'd discover it days later when Mom brought it up.

On the other hand, your emotions and perceptions can also cloud reality when it comes to someone who is selfishly taking advantage of you. Maybe your boyfriend is continually minimizing your worries about work and instead spending all of your time together complaining about how his supervisor is a real prick for getting on him about taking five extra minutes on his lunch break.

When you don't admit that someone is being selfish, it's very difficult to address the problem in a helpful manner. In order to most effectively evaluate a situation it can be helpful to sit and make a list of evidence to help you visualize what's actually going on. It can also be helpful to find a trusted third party to bounce your impressions off of and help you to ask yourself the right questions.

Take Care of Yourself

This shouldn't have to be said, but sadly it does. Take care of your needs. Often, selfish people will demand more of you than is healthy for you to give them. Whether they realize they are doing this to you or not, continuing to allow them to sap all of your energy and time will impair your judgment in other aspects of your life as well.

My friend Anna lived with a roommate a couple of years ago who refused to pay rent for various reasons—he was focusing on finding himself, he was going through a painful breakup, he was sick with a cold or mono or some unknown new ailment that no one could seem to find a cure for. I asked her if the unknown ailment without a cure was laziness.

Anna had sighed. "I feel so bad for him. I know he's going through stuff, but I've had to pick up like a million shifts at the factory to keep up with rent and utilities. I don't know how much longer I can keep this schedule up. The whole point of having a roommate was so I didn't have to do this." Dark bags hung under her eyes.

We sipped coffee at her place on one of her rare afternoons off. Her hands shook from fatigue. I'd already offered to call off our hangout so she could sleep, but she had protested harder than I had expected.

"I need advice," she said. "Am I being unreasonable for wanting to kick him out and find a roommate who can actually help me pay? I'm so angry, but I don't want to be unkind."

"How long has he been living here?" I asked.

"Four months."

"That's way too long to expect someone who isn't your family to take care of you."

"He doesn't have any family in the area," she said. "And I know how hard it can be to make it on your own, because I've been there."

"No, Anna. You were never in his position. Even at your lowest, you were waiting tables in a crummy diner and buying me groceries when you could while you stayed on my couch for three weeks. Has he offered to pay for anything?"

"He can't. He doesn't have a job."

"Then there's the problem. If you were a landlord, he would have been out on his ear three months ago. Give him a notice. You're exhausted all the time because of him. You live on ramen and cheap hotdogs because of him. You never get to go out with your friends or do your volunteer work because of him. It's not fair of him to expect you to keep living this way, and the longer you let him take advantage of you, the more entitled he will feel."

She sighed. "I know," she said. "I just needed someone to tell me that I'm not crazy for feeling that way."

If someone's selfishness is keeping you from being able to meet your basic needs and hugely cutting into your happiness, then it's time to take action.

Stop Enabling

If, like my friend Anna, someone is taking advantage of you and running you ragged, solving the problem might be as simple as stopping enabling them. The longer you help them continue in their selfish behaviors, the harder you will ultimately make life for yourself.

I used to be bullied in high school by the most popular girl in my grade, a girl I deeply wanted to impress and be noticed by. She would say mean things to me in school and spread rumors about me, like that I had fatty side boobs and that I had once made out with the grossest boy in the class. They were lies, but everyone believed her. After weeks of cowering in the bathroom during lunch period like a high school movie cliché, I finally worked up the nerve to ask her to stop.

She laughed at me and told me that she would stop on one condition: I had to write all of her papers for her for the rest of the school year. I agreed. Writing papers was easy for me, and I was clever enough to know not to get her too high of a grade so no one would ever suspect that she didn't write them herself.

That school year ended, and the next one began. I continued to write her papers for her, fearing the rumors she would spread about me if I didn't. I made friends with Anna, who was funny and smart and nice to me. She learned that I wrote papers for the popular girl and asked me why I didn't just stop. I explained the situation to her.

"Really?" Anna said. "I know it sucked because you were a freshman, and you thought she was so cool, but no one really cared what she said about you. You're enabling her." She had just learning the word "enabling" from her grandmother, who had accused her mother of enabling her older brother by letting him live in the basement without a job at twenty-five years old.

I realized that Anna was right. I informed the popular girl that I was no longer writing papers for her. In addition, I told her that if she started spreading rumors about me, I would show the principal proof that she had cheated on every paper she ever turned in for the past year.

She never bothered me again.

If you find that you are constantly doing favors or bailing someone out of their debt or other recurring problems that they aren't willing or able to deal with, then you might be inadvertently feeding their selfishness. Stop it. It's called tough love. Or if you don't, in fact, love them, then it's called Tough, and that's a valuable lesson, too.

Don't Stoop

Don't stoop to the same level as someone who is being selfish toward you. Sometimes the kneejerk reaction to selfishness is to be selfish and demanding in return, thinking that you are teaching them a lesson.

I can't count the number of times I spent in passive aggressive determination to teach my older brother a lesson for eating all of my breakfast cereal by eating all of his, even if I didn't feel like eating it, or having a loud fake phone conversation about how selfish he was outside of his bedroom door while he was listening to the country music I hated so much. These are petty examples. If I had stopped to honestly evaluate the situation, I might have seen that these weren't deliberate attempts to make my life miserable. I would have also noted that if the country music was an attempt to selfishly make my life miserable, then telling my friends how selfish he was being only fed his amusement.

If a person is truly very self-centered, they won't see the lesson you are trying to give them; they will see you acting irrationally, which won't solve your problem.

Don't Dote

A selfish person thinking only of themselves will be pleased by doting comments and take them as encouragement to continue their selfish behavior.

A friend monopolizing your attention about a trivial matter with a coworker when you have a giant presentation to prepare for the next day that will determine the trajectory of your startup company and its investors will feel encouraged to continue their complaining when you say things like, "You poor thing," and, "I don't understand why people are so mean to you all the time either. You clearly don't deserve that."

The best thing you can do to self-absorbed people is to starve them of attention. If he is a narcissist or is always making critical comments about himself or others, sometimes the best way to get him to stop is to ignore him. When he notices that his critiques go unacknowledged, he might come around to making more relevant or helpful comments instead.

Another thing you can do to avoid doting is to respond with a dose of reality. You might say, "Yeah, that's life," or, "We've all got to learn to suck it up and deal with that stuff. You're not the exception," instead of feeding their self-pity meter.

Change the Subject

Especially when in the presence of an Inconsiderate or a Narcissist, it may be difficult to steer the conversation away from them and their problems or life stories. Sometimes, you have to straight up change the subject on them.

Talk about things that interest you. This works best if you are in a group. For the subject change to be most effective, choose a subject of conversation that will appeal to the majority of your group.

There's no rule that says you have to let the most self-absorbed person in the group do all of the talking or choose all of the conversation topics. The Narcissist might become bored and leave, but that's so much the better, as this will open the floor for the other members of your group to participate and have a nice time together.

Set A Limit

Maybe a good friend is simply going through a phase in which she thinks and talks constantly about herself. Maybe she is using her tough situation as an excuse to let you pay for all of her meals and treat her to gifts that you don't entirely mean to buy for her. Perhaps you don't want to lose her as a friend, but she's currently reeking destruction on your pocket book and sapping your mental energy. It might be time to set limits for yourself on how much time you will spend with her every week.

You know what you can take. If you can't take spending every evening after work with someone, then don't make yourself. It might be better for your relationship in the long run if you distance yourself from the selfish friend before your entire friendship is replaced with contempt.

You might feel guilty, but there's nothing wrong with limiting the amount of time you spend with someone. Sometimes a person's level of selfishness can be so toxic that it's having a huge negative effect on your own mental or physical health. These are the kinds of people you *should* actively seek to spend less of your time with, as they consistently drain your resources without giving you anything in return.

Find Better Friends

I've mentioned a few times that my friend
Zelda is cynical. That's because she grew up in a
rough neighborhood with friends who were more
like tentative allies than buddies. They had each
other's backs only until something more
promising came along. Zelda told me that one
time her best friend ditched her when she
tripped on her way home from school and the
gang from the next neighborhood started yelling
at them.

Lying alone on the ground with a bloody
knee, Zelda told them every lie she could think of
to get them to leave her alone, including the fact
that she had seen them graffiti the back of the
liquor store and could call the cops on them. She
said it was a lucky guess, but they hesitated and
left after only giving her a swift kick in the side.

After a childhood of friends who never
had her back, Zelda finally got out of her
hometown and went to college, where she met
friends who thought she was funny and valued

her for the person she was and not just for the physical safety her presence may or may not contribute to. She hasn't talked to any of her childhood friends since, though a couple of them have tried to contact her and beg money off of her over the years.

Sometimes the best thing you can do to fend off selfish people is to fill your life with people who genuinely care about you. A person who genuinely cares about you will be able to curb their selfish inclinations to help you out when you're in a jam or compliment you on a bad day or let you be the center of attention when it's your turn.

End the relationship

The flip side of finding new friends is that sometimes you have to make room for them by eliminating the toxic ones. Sometimes this is the best option, especially when it comes to perpetual narcissists. Until a selfish person decides to change, there's nothing you can do to fix him, and it's only making you tired or crazy trying.

CHAPTER FIVE: TOXIC PERSONALITIES

While some level of selfishness is present in one hundred percent of humans and often fluctuates based on life events and stages of life, there are numerous toxic personality flaws that are less all encompassing but every bit as lethal, and perhaps even more so.

Recent studies by German scientists at Friedrich Schiller University have shown that negative emotions, like those present when we are in the company of truly toxic people, create a stress response inside our brains that can have a permanent negative impact on the hippocampus, the part of the brain that deals with memory and reasoning. So basically, toxic people not only make you feel miserable, but they literally destroy parts of your brain (Bradberry, 2016).

This chapter is meant to take you beyond selfishness and give you a peak into other toxic personality types that can darken your reality and bring it down around you in flames— metaphorical or literal.

The Egotist

The Egotist lives a life of complete arrogance, believing herself to be superior to everyone around her. She will intimidate or belittle you long before she will treat you with respect. Beyond being a narcissist, she thrives on doing everything she can to increase her sense of self-worth and self-importance in large part by doing everything in her power to drag others down.

An old office rival from my post college days was an egotist. He wanted the same promotion that I did, but unlike me, he had no qualms about pointing out every failure I had in front of everyone and, and particularly the boss. He deliberately lost my files and told everyone that I hadn't done my part in the project. He talked himself up to all of the supervisors, carefully weaving in the fact that he always got his work done on time, unlike me and some other coworkers he thought might turn into his competition at the last second. He went so far as to steal my work and put his name on it.

Confronting him did no good. He simply lied or told me that it wasn't his fault I couldn't keep track of my files.

In that circumstance, good prevailed when the boss caught him pushing one of my files into the trash, just as I'd explained happened on a regular basis. I won the promotion, and my first order of business was to transfer my egotist rival to a department in a different building.

The Envious

The Envious person mopes at your success and delights in your failures. Their own success is less than they deserve, and yours is too much for them to handle.

I once met a woman in a doctor's waiting room. At the time, she had a rash on her face, and I was there with a broken arm and had a giant gash on my face from an accident with some heavy office equipment I'd stubbornly tried to move by myself. We were fast friends. We bonded over our mutual face blemishes and exchanged numbers.

The strange thing about my new friend was that she was delighted by my blemish, but she became sulky when I told her that it looked like there wouldn't be much visible scarring from the injury. Every time I told her something negative that was happening in my life, she perked up, and every time I got a promotion or started a new relationship, she never seemed happy for me.

I tried quizzing her about this peculiarity, and she told me, "It's just that I don't feel like it's fair that I never have good things like that happen to me."

I pointed out that she was married to a great guy, had two little kids who adored her, and a job she liked.

She sighed and instead threw out some petty good thing that I had accomplished and say, "But I never get things like that."

Her constant desire to bring me down in my high moments and her almost blatant delight in my breakups and stolen identity and coffee stain on my white pants drove a wedge between us. I gradually stopped returning her calls. A real friend can set aside rampant envy long enough to be happy for you when you're happy and sad for you when you're sad. A chronically envious person is toxic and will only bring you down.

The Pretentious

The pretentious person is your best friend when they need something and nowhere to be found when you need the favor returned. They are, essentially, a pretender. They will pretend to be your friend if it suits their needs and desires, but as soon as anything is required of them as per the basic friendship rule of reciprocity, they are too busy, too tired, too broke, too overwhelmed, to preoccupied, or any number of other excuses.

I once stayed up all night to help a friend move and was disappointed when he was in no way inclined to help me move when I needed help later that year. He told me he was busy that day. I asked if I could use his truck, and he said that he was using it that weekend. When I drove by his house on the way to my new place to sign the lease, I saw his truck in the driveway. Through the giant front windows in his living room, I saw him in his boxers playing video games on his sixty inch TV screen.

Obviously you can't expect that doing a favor for someone entitles you to a favor in return, but if you start to notice a pattern with a particular friend who constantly needs your help but is never available to give any to you when you need it, it might be time to start exercising your right to say no on occasion.

The Retrogressive

The Retrogressive is that old friend from high school who still wants you to get drunk and party the way you used to in the good old days whenever you're together. He's the chum who wants you to be stagnant in your life. When he says, "Don't ever change," he means it, and he will go to great lengths to be sure that you don't.

One of Zelda's childhood friends came to visit her once and tried to persuade Zelda to give her a lift so she could sell some good stuff in a neighborhood that was a little rough. Zelda, knowing exactly what kind of "good stuff" this was, said no. The friend became angry and walked there by herself instead.

The friend ended up getting busted in possession of drugs and hauled to jail. The friend tried to incriminate Zelda, but Zelda stood her ground. She had refused to aid in the delivery when asked, and she had not known that the friend sleeping on her couch had brought drugs along. The police let Zelda go.

The Judge

The Judge is the judgmental person who criticizes everything you do and never hands out praise. She is quick to assume the worst about you and your intentions. She is a terrible listener and even worse at differentiating between your intentions and her own perceptions.

One of my friends has a judgmental brother who is an expert at selective understanding. I might make an innocuous comment about how annoyed I am about a certain presidential candidate's blatantly racist comments, and suddenly he's telling me that I'm a heartless person devoid of a conscience and the reason why women shouldn't be allowed to have opinions. He's easily the most judgmental person I've ever met, and every time I happen to be in the same room with him, he takes pains to let me know how heartily he disapproves of me and my beliefs.

The Judge doesn't appreciate or respect differences of opinion; he uses them as ammunition to feed his own narrow opinion and point out how ridiculous everyone who doesn't agree with him is.

The Control Freak

The Control Freak is a master manipulator. This person will go to great lengths to get you to do his bidding, micromanage you, or persuade you to think, feel, or act in the way she wishes.

These people may control you with force, but more commonly, they will control you through a façade of friendship. They know you well—what you hate, what you like, what makes you laugh—and they know exactly what it will take to get you to do what they want you to do.

The Control Freak goes far beyond the well-meaning friend who offers you pizza and beer to help her fix her toilet. The Control Freak will make you feel obligated to fix the toilet, the faucet, the wiggly step, the tile in the kitchen, and the water spot in the ceiling before you realize that you've signed away your day off to taking care of someone else's problems.

The Control Freak can make you feel guilty for pursuing your hobbies, make you blame yourself for bad things that have nothing to do with you, and all the while keep up the front that they are your friend.

The Liar

The Liar tells lies to get her way in any and every situation. She sees lying as an easy way out of most scrapes and troubles. Lying deflects the blame from her and places it on others. The Liar doesn't necessarily know the distinction between harmless white lies and harmful lies. All she knows is that her lies get her exactly what she wants from you at your expense. She's so accustomed to lying, and the lies slip out of her mouth so easily, that she may not even realize that she's telling lies.

My mother's childhood friend had a propensity to lie about everything. A lot of the time, she didn't seem to have any real reason to be lying, but for some reason the lie slipped out more easily than the truth for her. Mom had asked if she was going to a neighborhood party, and she had said yes, even though she didn't plan on going. When Mom asked where she had been, she said that she had to take care of a sick child, but the child in question had been at a friend's house, so she made up another story to explain herself.

The lies kept coming, and by the time the truth came out, she had maddened her husband, estranged her children, and had the neighbors beating down her door demanding that she give back whatever it was she had stolen from— expensive liquor, jewelry, shoes. It turned out that lying wasn't her only problem. She was also a gifted kleptomaniac, a borderline alcoholic, and was wanted in Arizona for suspected manslaughter for a hit and run she must have done when she said she was on vacation in the Bahamas. When all of this hit the fan, her former employer started looking into records and discovered that on top of everything else, she had possibly embezzled almost $50,000 from his private practice over the course of ten years.

My mother was beside herself when all of this finally started coming out. "I had no idea she was in so much trouble. No wonder she felt she had to lie about everything."

"I think you're giving her too much credit," I said. "I think all the lying is what got her into this mess to begin with."

A person who compulsively lies about everything, no matter how big or small, is a toxic personality that you can't trust. The habit of lying is often so deeply ingrained in them that they can't stop even if they want to, and they will eventually bring down everyone around them in their web of lies and deceit.

The Gossip

The gossip, talks about others in an unflattering light behind their back, usually for the purpose of raising himself in others' esteem. Contrary to popular opinion, gossiping isn't just a women's game. Men do it to.

Back when Anna was still pulling night shifts in the factory, she used to work with a bunch of guys. During break, they'd sit around the break table trashing the supervisor or whichever guy got up to go to the bathroom or go outside to smoke. The activity was a sort of rapport building activity, in which one guy would rag on the absent party in the filthiest language he could think of, and the next guy to speak would try to top that. It may have been an overall more raunchy and competitive exchange, but it was still gossip.

Anytime a person is taking advantage of another person's absence from the group in order to trash talk them, spread unsavory information, or manipulate public opinion regarding them, it's gossip.

A Gossip, afraid that you are climbing the social ladder too quickly in the neighborhood you just moved into, might mention to another neighbor in passing that she heard that you got pregnant on purpose so that your husband had to leave his estate to the child, and, by proxy, you when he died or left you. By the time you show up to the next social function, half of the neighborhood is whispering about you and the other half is actively turning up their noses at you.

While most of us have been guilty of doing this at one point or another, the chronic gossip does it constantly. She is happiest when she is tearing someone down, and if she ever feels guilty for doing it, it's only because she got caught, and now everyone thinks ill of her.

The Dementor

This parasitic person will take everything you give them and then some until you are sucked dry. This person is very much like the selfish leech from chapter three. The primary difference is that, while the leech may be going through a phase, the Dementor is a lifelong parasite. He is more than a selfish person; like the Dementors from J.K. Rowling's Harry Potter series, he can make a room cold and desolate just by entering it.

The Dementor will take your soul and leave only the shell of your body behind, leaving you feeling emotionally ravaged every time you are together. Often, he does this through his chronic pessimism. He is skilled at making joyful celebrations seem worthless and sad and seemingly benign events seem somehow frightening and cruel.

My friend, Zelda, can be cynical, but the Dementor goes beyond basic cynicism.

The Dementor is that friend who shows up on your doorstep in a dark mood, eats all your food, insults your home and your family, complains about all of her problems, begs for help, and then shoots down every solution you offer. You can never comfort a Dementor, because they warp everything you say into something depressing or provide such strong objections that all the logic in the world can't seem to undo them. She overstays her welcome, turns a good day sour by her presence, and is always ready with a negative quip.

A study done at Notre Dame University showed that college students with overly negative roommates tended to become negative and even depressed over the course of the school year while living with theses negative people (Bradberry, 2016). Negative energy is something to beware of, as its reach tends to be deeper and longer lasting than positive energy. If you spend significant time with a Dementor friend, your mental health could be at stake.

The Victim

The Victim is never at fault and doesn't accept responsibility for negative actions.

Here is my disclaimer: I'm not talking about people who truly are victims here. If someone tells you she has been raped, attacked in a violent crime, or abused in some way, you should take her seriously, because being truly victimized is a serious thing. The true victim is not the kind of person I'm talking about here.

The toxic victim personality is the person who is always claiming to be the victim in a situation and will blame anyone but himself for it, even when it was clearly his fault. He might have been fiddling with the radio while he rear-ended someone, but he will blame it on the soft brakes in the car he's borrowing from his parents or on a fly buzzing in front of him or on the driver next to her giving him a dirty look for no apparent reason. He will say whatever he has to say to make it not his fault, at least in his own eyes. He is a master at justifying—so much so that he usually believes that he is telling the truth.

I once dated a guy—I'll call him Dick—who was always the victim. When we met, he was being aggressively pursued by a crazy coworker who had decided to attach herself to him and wear him down until he agreed to go out with her. When the coworker noticed that Dick and I had become friends, she switched her tactic and attached herself to me instead. She was my own personal Dementor, and she made me believe that Dick really was a victim. We bonded over our mutual disgust at this coworker and eventually started dating each other.

The more time I spent with Dick, the more I began to realize that he had a lot of bad things like that happen to him, and he always had a reason for why they weren't his fault. Like a good girlfriend, I always took his side and listened to what he had to say.

One of his constant complaints was that he was stuck in a dead end job. Every time I tried to encourage him to get out an apply for a different job, he had an excuse for why this was impossible—his computer was broken, his internet connection was bad, he was exhausted from working his current job because the boss expected him to do the work of two people, there were some experiences in his past that disqualified him from working in the field he really wanted to be in, and the list went on.

The longer we were together, the less patience I had for his excuses and constant victim mentality. I was sympathetic about the crummy things that had happened to him in the past, but I was beginning to have a problem with the fact that he didn't seem willing to do anything that would help him move on from the past and build a better future for himself.

I learned that there's sometimes a very fine line between a true victim and a person who refuses to move on from a victimized past and make himself better. The toxic Victim is one who sees all of the fault in others and has an inability to move on from life's unfairness.

The Twisted

The Twisted person seeks pleasure at your misery and will go to lengths to make you more miserable. If he can't make you miserable, get something from you, or otherwise make you feel terrible, then he has no purpose for you.

The nice thing about the Twisted, is that they are a lot easier to spot than most of the other toxic personality types. These are the people who will blatantly use and abuse others.

Remember when I talked about Helen's ex-boyfriend in Chapter Three? He was a twisted guy. He'd cheat on her and blame her for it. He would get her drunk in order to have sex with her and then persuade her that it was all her fault when she woke up. Sometime he hit her in order to get her to agree with him. Whenever she cried or expressed her dismay, he laughed at her. Every time she tried to break up with him, he had some manipulative reason why she couldn't—he was the best she could do, no other man would ever want her, he would tell everyone he knew that she had been a controlling bitch who made him lose his job, he would burn her house down, he would rough up her little sister. He had innumerable reasons for her to stay with him, and, for a while, they were enough.

Sometimes twisted people are cunning and hard to catch in the act, but usually a few prods is all it takes to bring their deceptions and cruelty down around them and reveal them as the twisted maniacs they are.

CHAPTER SIX: FENDING OFF THE DARK SIDE

In 1961, researcher Stanley Milgram performed a series of experiments that sought to understand why a reprehensible killing spree like the Holocaust could succeed, given that so many of us are horrified by the atrocities committed against other humans during World War II.

In one of the experiments test subjects were commanded by an authority figure to press a button that would administer volts of electricity to an unseen victim on the other side of a wall. Those who pressed the button heard screams of torture and agony coming from the victim. The authority figure would then ask them to press another button to administer an even higher voltage.

It's easy to fold your hands in self-righteous shock and think, "I would never do something like that!"

But the study showed that two thirds of Milgram's eight hundred test subjects were persuaded to continue pressing the buttons.

The Stanford Prison Experiment of 1971 produced similarly dark results. A bunch of test subjects were assigned roles as prisoners and prison guards. Zimbardo, the researcher, wanted to look at the way different personality types played into abuse in prison.

The first day of the experiment passed relatively uneventfully. Then some of the prisoners formed a blockade with their beds and refused to come out of their cell or listen to the guards. Guards who weren't on duty were called in to help stop the revolt taking place. Some of the prisoners were attacked with fire extinguishers.

After this, the guards began to wage psychological warfare on the inmates. They set up a privileged cell to reward the prisoners who hadn't participated in the revolt, but the privileged prisoners went on a hunger strike. To punish the prisoners, the guards took away mattresses, refused to let insubordinate prisoners empty their urine buckets, and forced them to be naked in order to degrade them.

After 36 hours, one prisoner had gone crazy and was sent out, and the other prisoners started circulating a rumor that he would come back with a posse and break the rest of them free. Even Zimbardo, the experimenter and warden had become so engrossed in the reality of the experiment by this point that he was worried this might actually happen and moved the prison to a different floor of the university.

All participants in the experiment became so entrenched in their new identities that some of them seemed to forget that it wasn't real, even offering to forego their daily payment for participation in order to gain parole.

Designed to last two weeks, the experiment was cut short after six days when Zimbardo's girlfriend objected to the rancid conditions and blatant psychological and physical abuse that was taking place in the prison. The dark reality was that it was actually so easy to get caught up in a pretend reality that they acted in ways that went contrary to their rational thoughts and beliefs. The even darker reality was that of the dozens of people who came to the fake prison to see the experiment in action, Zimbardo's girlfriend was the only person who objected to the experiment on ethical grounds.

Both of these experiments have continued to rock the psychological boat decades later, as researchers have continued to explore the behaviors associated with the compliant and abusive test subjects,

Further studies done on the methodology and results of these experiments have revealed some fascinating insight into the ways in which people resist authority and resist the pulls of an alternate reality. The rest of this chapter will explore the techniques used by the noncompliant test subjects, particularly those in the Milgram study, to prolong taking action and, eventually, to halt the experiment.

Based on Milgram's recordings of his experiments, both the compliant and noncompliant alike tended to use many of the same inadvertent techniques to try to make it stop. The difference between the compliant and noncompliant was that the noncompliant had a tendency to use them earlier in the experiment and in a more diverse manner, mixing and matching techniques in order to bolster their own confidence and stance.

Techniques Used to Fight Obedience in a Dark World

The following list isn't numerical. When you need to resist a would-be authority figure you can use these in any order to do everything from buy you time to throw the other person off their game. These aren't just used on authority figures; you can also use them when you are in situations with selfish or toxic people who are trying to persuade you to do something that believe is wrong or that you find to be unappetizing.

Silence or Hesitation

"You don't even have to do anything else. I just want you to change that one little number. That hardly counts as doing anything," Kevin, my supervisor said. He wanted me to alter one tiny number, which would divert several thousand dollars every month from the company's revenue account to his own secret account that was labeled to look like one of the company's special projects funds.

I didn't want to do it, though he could fire me for insubordination if I didn't obey. The moment stretched long as I gathered my thoughts. I could get fired for this. I could get fired and never get another job in accounting as long as I lived. Not to mention the jail time.

Kevin had been confident I would agree when he approached me. He knew I didn't love what this company stood for. He'd assumed it was a no-brainer to come to me. But the longer I hesitated, the more he began to sweat, and I realized only later that letting him sweat was putting the power back in my own hands.

Hesitating won't always put the power in your hands. In fact, sometimes it's important to act quickly, as in flight or fight situations. In most interpersonal interactions, however, allowing yourself a few seconds to think before speaking is a good idea, as it allows you to check your words before you say them. In dark situations, it's best to have your wits about you. Hesitating gives you a moment to collect those wits before you act.

Groaning or Sighing

Your roommate asks you to be his getaway driver while he makes a drop in a dangerous neighborhood. This is not the first time he's asked you to do this for him. You've agreed in the past, but you're really trying to turn your life around and leave that kind of stuff behind.

You groan.

The groan, like the hesitation, buys you another second, and it relays your reluctance to participate in the plan. It's an audible reinforcement of the fact that you don't want to participate.

Laughing

Many of Milgram's test subjects laughed nervously when they were told to administer the electric volts. It wasn't that they thought the request was funny but rather more like sighing or groaning. They're shocked by the request, and it's a way to audibly pause.

You might also use a laugh as a means of bringing the requester down few a pegs. For example, if a sick elderly man's son asks you to add a few drops of poison to his morning coffee, telling you that if you don't, he'll make your life a living hell, you might try a round of confident laughter to throw him off. You might make him think that you thought he was joking. You might make him believe that you know something he doesn't know. Suddenly, he's uncertain.

Speaking to the Victim

Many of Milgram's noncompliant test subjects asked the victim how they were feeling and gave them a say in the matter. The victims' responses bolstered their resolve not to continue inflicting the pain on them. In the case of the Milgram study, speaking to the victim seemed to begin as a method of prolonging the eventuality of performing the task the authority figure had commanded of them. It likely served the dual purpose of reinforcing the test subject's gut instincts that they should not be obeying.

Perhaps a certain factory owner is petitioning a legislator to lift an environmental law, so they can save money in disposing of the factory's waste. They make the argument that lifting the law would free up funding to create a hundred new jobs in the community. The legislator doesn't like the idea of allowing the factory to freely pollute the river and air. She goes to the adjacent neighborhoods and talks with the people who live there and would be affected by the pollution. The people who live there testify that the air already smells of refuse and that the river is already so polluted in their area that it's too toxic to touch.

Hearing the perspectives of the community members helps the legislator solidify her own perspective on the matter. More pollution in a community already full of factory pollution would create living conditions that were uninhabitable.

Speaking to the victims can be like forming an alliance. Find mouthpieces for your own opinions who will speak for you without you having to put the words in their mouths. Sometimes this is the most persuasive way to get an authority figure or opponent to back down from something that might be unethical.

Telling the Authority to Fix It

During my brief stint in retail, a customer had had an intestinal explosion all over the women's bathroom, and the manager called me to fix it. I went in to check it out, and not only was the whole situation worse than described, but it was clearly of a magnitude that a professional cleaning service ought to have been called in to deal with it for personal and public health reasons.

"You're the only female employee in the store, so you have to go in there and fix it," the manager told me.

After taking one look at the mess, I immediately left the bathroom, slapped a closed sign on the door, and told the manager that this was his problem to figure out. This is a trivial example, but the technique applies whether someone wants you to perform beyond the scope of your job description and pay grade or whether they want you to take the fallout for their money laundering and serve their jail time.

Sometimes if someone wants something done, they'll have to do it themselves instead of delegating to others. If you experience someone trying to rope you into their unsavory plan or hidden agenda against your will, telling them that this is their problem to deal with can be very effective.

Refusing

Of all of these techniques, flat refusal is the first that probably comes to mind for most of us. The noncompliant participants in Milgram's study eventually flat out refused to do what the authority figure asked them to do. They said that they were unable or unwilling to press the button to inflict pain on another human.

Let's go back to the example of me and Kevin and the proposed number fudge. I'm hesitating; he's starting to sweat. Finally, I say, "That would be fraud, and I won't have any part in it. In fact, I can turn you in for this, and I'm probably going to." He wheedles and begs, realizing that his fate rests in my hands. Then, he fires me on the spot and scours all of the company records until there's no trace of me having worked there.

Note that a successful refusal does not guarantee a happy ending. A lot of the time, if a person with a dark agenda can't get you to do his bidding, he'll get rid of you and find someone else. That's a chance you take with refusal, but not refusing is often to place your own liberty at stake.

Refusal can look drastically different in different situations. Sometimes it's an outright no. Sometimes the refusal has to be gentler. Refusing an influential friend or coworker might involve composing a tasteful note explaining that you're flattered that they thought of you but stating clearly and succinctly why you can't or won't meet their request.

Make sure that you are evaluating your situation accurately and that you understand the implications of what they are asking you to do. Maybe the request is not as bad as you think it is, but if it's every bit as unsavory, make sure you can clearly and firmly state why you're not going to do it.

Diversify Techniques

Statistically, the participants in Milgram's experiment who succeeded in noncompliance were the ones who used a combination of the above tactics. Sometimes picking a strategy and sticking with it is successful if the authority figure you are saying no to isn't very intimidating and the stakes aren't very high. Maybe the pastor at your church is asking you to lead a prayer group. You might hesitate, and he might immediately accept your hesitation as a no and go ask someone else instead. No big deal.

But when the authority figure is someone who could exercise dangerous power over you, simply hesitating for a long time or saying no a bunch of times might not defer his determination to get you to do his bidding.

Each technique you use reinforces your own perspective and determination. Use silence, say no, state reasons, ask for the victims' perspective, cough or groan. All of these buy you more time, and with each new tactic used, your chances of successfully enforcing your stance increase.

A colleague asks you to help him write a paper about a topic you don't feel comfortable with. He's offered to pay you for your time. You might hesitate at first, telling him you'll have to think about it. Upon further thought, you still don't want to do it, so you compose a note.

When crafting a "No" message, keep three things in mind. First, be prompt. A person who has asked you for a favor won't forget that she asked you, so don't put it off and hope the request disappears. Second, briefly explain why you can't do whatever it is that they've asked of you—you're too busy, you aren't qualified, etc. Don't go into a lot of detail. The more details you give, the more apt they will be to try to find the loopholes in your explanation. Keeping it short keeps the miniscule details of your life from their scrutiny. Thirdly, you might suggest another option to deflect the attention from yourself. Suggest someone else who might be interested or suggest another course of action. This works best when the person you are resisting is a friend or friendly acquaintance.

If you need to refuse a stranger or someone less close to you, the best way to say no is often just to say no. Today's culture tries to, and largely succeeds at, making us feel guilty for saying no. People don't say no very often. It's, "I would, but..." or, "If it were any other day..." Statements like these leave room for persuasion. If by, "Not this time," you really mean, "Never," then make that clear, and the person will be less likely to ask you again in the future.

Remember, if you feel that saying yes would be morally repulsive to you or compromises you or your loved ones in some way, then you shouldn't have to feel guilty for straight up saying no. Also keep in mind that sometimes, "I don't want to," is a valid reason for not doing something.

Starting Early

In Milgram's experiment, the people who were the least compliant were the ones who started their objections and hesitations early on. This is where hesitation can flounder. Don't wait too long to employ one of the other tactics or your chances at succeeding could go down.

Most people don't give in to something immoral, illegal, or unethical immediately. Most people will employ some sort of resistance tactic. The sooner you do it, and the more of them you use, the better.

Sustaining Resistance

Where most people fail when it comes to resisting is in the sustenance of the resistance. You have to be able to sustain your objections even while the authority figure counters your reasons or remains steadfast in her demand.

In order to sustain resistance, you might do any of a number of things. You can mentally prepare yourself for a potential conflict by preparing counterarguments in advance. People who have counterarguments prepared are less likely to blindly follow what someone says. Another thing you can do is think about the people who would support your decision to say no. What would they say? Let their perspectives bolster your own.

The nonconforming participants in Milgram's study sustained their no and eventually demanded to leave the experiment, showing that sticking to your guns is the best way to come out of a situation with your values intact.

CONCLUSION: TOGETHER IN A DARK WORLD

"People inspire you, or they drain you—pick them wisely," said Hans F. Hansen.

The world is a dark place full of emotional piracy and people who are out to use you, cheat you, and lie to you. Even people who claim to be your friends can turn out to be anything but, which, I think, might be the darkest thing of all.

In a dark world, there are only a few choices you can make concerning your own perspective. You can let the darkness swallow you, you can live a life of skepticism closed off from everyone around you, or you can find the few people in the world who genuinely care about you and have your back.

No one is good all the time, but neither are most people entirely bad.

I'm scribbling this as a party I'm hosting is starting to pick up this evening. Anna is talking about some jerk she met who tried to get her to take her shirt of on the subway, and Ben is threatening to beat him up if he ever sees the creep. They start laughing at Anna's description of him—he was wearing a yellow and orange striped scarf that looked like Big Bird squashed in a trash compactor, and his sleeve tattoo was of a woman's face.

"Clearly harassing chicks on subways is not his worst mistake," Ben says. "I wonder whose face is tattooed on his ass." Several of my friends laugh.

Helen is telling Zelda that her new dress looks great, and Zelda is twirling with a bright smile plastered across her usually serious face. She would be a lot more cynical if it weren't for us. Helen would be stuck with a good-for-nothing cheating boyfriend if it weren't for us. Anna would be letting freeloaders walk all over her and take advantage of her generous nature if it weren't for us.

And me. I would be desolate without them. They laugh with me, cry with me, pick me up when I'm feeling sorry for myself, give me their two cents whether I ask for it or not, and show up on my doorstep with drinks and appetizers ready to party for no particular reason other than it's Friday and we're alive. They're not perfect, but they are good people.

They're calling me away from my notebook and pouring me a drink. I'm proposing a toast—to good friends who sustain you through a dark reality. May we all live happily ever after, giving darkness the metaphorical finger.

Bibliography

Barncard, C. (2015, January 09). Infamous study
    of humanity's 'dark side' may actually
    show how to keep it at bay. Retrieved
    April 20, 2016, from
    http://news.wisc.edu/infamous-study-of-
    humanitys-dark-side-may-actually-show-
    how-to-keep-it-at-bay/

Bradberry, T. (n.d.). 10 Toxic People You Should
    Avoid At All Costs. Retrieved April 20,
    2016, from
    http://www.talentsmart.com/articles/10-
    Toxic-People-You-Should-Avoid-At-All-
    Costs-1858605350-p-1.html

www.ingramcontent.com/pod-product-compliance
Lightning Source LLC
Chambersburg PA
CBHW020542290526
45786CB00002B/997